CHARACTER

How to Strengthen It

D. STARKE

Psycho Information Technologies
New Delhi - 110009

Character : How to Strengthen it-D. Sharke

First Indian Edition

ISBN - 978-81-924500-7-0

Published by
Psycho Information Technologies
B-6, Mukherjee Tower, Commercial Complex, Dr. Mukherjee Nagar, Delhi
Mob.: 08700413360
psychoinformationtechnologies@gmail.com

Typsetting & Cover Design by
J.K. Graphics, Bhajanpura, Delhi

Printed in India by
Milan Entreprises, Daryaganj, New Delhi - 110002

Pages: 109/Paper - 80gsm
Size of Book: 5.75X8.75

Rs. 499.00

Preface

To Samuel Smiles the crown and glory of life was Character. It is the noblest possession of man, constituting a rank in itself, and an estate in the general goodwill, dignifying every station, and exalting every position in society. Of itself Character is power and influence. Experience has taught us that the worth and the strength of a state depend upon the character of its men rather than on the form of its institutions. Just as the letters of the alphabet enable us to spell *reputation,* so do the actions, looks, and words of a man enable us to read his true *character.* Character is what one is; reputation is what one is thought to be. A man's character being himself must be molded by himself alone. In this work the Author, taking as his motto, "The man who can master himself can easily control events and man," teaches his readers how to strengthen character. He does this by explaining what constitutes strength of character, what this wonderful power can achieve, and how it may be acquired and utilized to best advantage.

Schopenhauer, whose cynical criticism gives voice to the bitterness of his heart against the world's whole artificial life, found time to teach us that men best show their character in trifles when they are not on their guard. "It is in insignificant matters," said he, "and in the simplest habits, that we often see the boundless egotism which pays no regard to the feelings of others, and denies nothing to itself." All the petty vexations of life serve their purpose in training us in moral discipline; these provide the severest test of character. There are many men who could face great dangers with calmness and resignation, yet who, if they be taken off their guard and their will be opposed, or their efforts thwarted, fly into uncontrollable passion. A man of character never allows the sun to set on his wrath, nor does he permit it to rise on his temerity. In these pages one is taught by a master-hand how the appetites and passions must be controlled to develop that calm force which is a factor necessary to self-domination, and how such physical ills as may arise from nervous affections, enervating forces, fear, etc., are to be overcome.

Nothing is left to chance. The body must be brought into harmony with the mind in every effort made to acquire patience and perseverance. Exercises for the development, both temperamental and physical, of character are provided in separate series. Impulsiveness of thought leads to impulsiveness of action; therefore, the reader is taught to control his impulses; to check irritability; and to cultivate that calm which permits one to concentrate one's powers, to use them advantageously in moments of excitement and stress. The exercises are designed to impart the quality of endurance, which is the keystone of character.

In the pages that follow, the Author leads the reader along the way he must travel to achieve success. The man who succeeds is he who saw his object in early life and never lost sight of it. "Genius," Bulwer tells us, "is but fine observation strengthened by fixity of purpose." Every man who is stedfastly resolute and a vigilant observer can attain success. Strength of character is resolution. Resolve to do something, and it will be done. Napoleon once said, "The truest wisdom is a resolute determination." The man of strong character is he who achieves success in business. His forcefulness is sustained by foresight, prudence, discernment, reason, logic, and clear thinking.

In the home, where one must learn to bear and forbear, strength of character is indispensable. There egotism invariably rules. Individual comfort is always in direct ratio to the efforts put forth to acquire it. We all seek some end, and to attain it must submit ourselves to the necessary discipline. There is need for strict attention to little things, for on these depend much of the peace and harmony of life. The man of strong will applies all the energies of his body and mind to every task that he undertakes and so avoids that failure which besets his weaker associates.

In business the one great difference between men—between the weak and the strong, the mean and the mighty—is one of character. It is not what a man makes but what a man does that he should give thought to. Let him think first of his character and then of his circumstances; for, character attracts but circumstances are dependent upon it. Some men, by combining great abilities with promising circumstances, have not only succeeded in acquiring distinction, but in creating characters that are the envy and admiration of mankind. Given a strong character, and energy, determination, and a fixt purpose will be found to attend it. These are the qualities that enable us to develop mentally, morally, and physically; that compel us to surmount all obstacles, to overcome all difficulties; and, finally, that teach us to resist temptation, and to bear the heaviest burdens cheerfully; the qualities that bring calmness before the storm, and fearlessness in the face of danger. He who heeds the advice given in the following pages will learn not only that character controls fame and fortune, but also that only the man who is master of himself can exercise a governing influence over his fellow men.

Contents

PART-I

CHARACTER: ITS ACQUISITION AND MASTERY

1

What Constitutes Strength of Character

Strength of character consists of an *ensemble* of qualities which endows its possessor with illimitable power over his instincts and his passions. It is the mastery of self at its highest expression: the application of the power of will to the multiplicity of temptations which constantly assail us. Further, it is the emancipation of the mind from the prejudices which enslave feeble souls, disdain for the petty annoyances whose repetition wears away an intermittent energy.

Strength of character aids us to elicit acts of the will with freedom, at the same time enabling us to bear up tinder reverses as well as to realize what we set out to accomplish. It is strength of character which enables us to consummate the act that we have fixt our choice upon; and thanks to it we not only can proceed surely in the choice of our resolutions, but are also equipped with the means to persevere in them.

At no former period whatsoever has strength of character been so indispensable as it is at the present time. Education, more widely diffused than ever, has refined human aspirations, given great scope to ambition, made more bitter the struggle for wealth. All feel themselves called, but how many are chosen? The world is filled with people who complain of their luck, instead of inquiring into its causes, while humbly admitting that it proceeds from frivolity and weakness. Anarchy of motive, giving in at the first impulse, hate of effort, concur to bring about defeat after defeat, and discouragement does the rest.

It is difficult to keep a foothold on a declivity; nevertheless, when one is sure of his way and determined to climb, he will reach the summit in spite of all obstacles. On the other hand, he, who instead of putting all his strength to the gripping of the rough ledges that might aid his ascent, permits himself to slip back without resistance, is pretty sure to roll to the bottom—lucky, indeed, if his fall be not fatal.

The obstacles we meet with are nothing less than our lower instincts, which disable us when we have not the strength to surmount them.

Strength of character is not a simple thing: it is the resultant of a complex effort to exert the will directed upon a single point—the mastery of self. We should, then, extend pity to the weak ones to whom we have just alluded, and who, alas, are legion; and at the same time we should seek to convince them of the truth.

Now, their principal defect consists in giving the preponderance to emotion over reason. They never make use of the will for the purpose of reflection; but finding themselves going wrong they bring their instincts into play: "I am wrong it is true, but what would you have? I was made that way and I can not make myself over again."

By declaring their conviction of the immovability of character they think to acquit themselves of the faults of fancy or momentary humor. They pretend that they are not able to change the character of the motives which are the foundation of volition in what concerns their habitual faults, and with this erroneous premise they allow themselves to go ahead, with a deplorable lack of all resistance.

It is true that we rarely succeed in completely transforming our nature, but through strength of character we succeed in neutralizing its manifestations up to the point where we no longer suffer from the exaggerations caused by ill-represt impulsiveness. It is only by self-restraint that we succeed in avoiding the error which impels us to obey the promptings of the moment, and thus condemns us to moral frailty and inconsistence.

The stereotyped saying that man is the slave of his passions has grown old only in appearance : it is as good as ever.

He who does not feel in himself the strength that character gives, must forego the triumph which comes from enfranchising oneself from irrational impulses.

The term "passions," which embraces inordinate, even sensual, appetites, is, perhaps, a little too pompous to apply to the daily inclinations and trivial acts which are suggested to us by weak character. But one should guard against making the mistake of those who only attach importance to great sentiments. Life is composed of a thousand little resolutions which, taken separately, may seem puerile enough, but combined form a formidable sheaf. Atrophy of will with regard to the envisaging of life is at the present time more than mere waste; it is a vice and an obstacle, something void in law.

We have now arrived at a point in education which permits a more detailed conception of moral personality. Social life is a field of labor for all, rich and poor alike, to whom indolence is repugnant. It is a field of action for each one.

For the poor it is a question of getting rich. For the rich it is a question of keeping what they have got.

You may say, perhaps, there are those who are modest and wise enough to be content with their lot; and this is possibly true as far as the second group is concerned, but if we admit it of the first we should have to include both under the denomination of the wise.

Let us remark, moreover, that both qualifications are embraced in the same category; there is no difference between a man who is satisfied with his lot and a sage. To be content with one's lot indicates strength of character of a very uncommon order. It implies a natural appreciation of one's own value, and at the same time self-sufficing strength without the need of foreign support or protection. To acquire this type of wisdom, however, excessive firmness of will is implied. This is the reason why we should include the modest, those *content with their lot,* and the wise as well, in the too-thin ranks of the army of the apostles of character.

What remain are the modest without further qualifications, and of these we shall have something to say. In the great social struggle that is going on he who keeps aloof is a shirker or a coward. He that shuns the combat must forego the triumph. It is only the militant who have a right to the joy of victory. The modest who are not also wise belong to the timid sort, a prey to all the ills of their defect; they conceal themselves under an appearance of disdain which is only too frequently a mask to conceal envious traits. The really modest struggle on in silence, without parade; but they take care to hold themselves aloof from the fracas and contribute, as do the wise, to the upbuilding of progress.

Character, therefore, is the resultant of an effort of will directed at itself. And, to acquire the power of manipulating, of "canalizing" this power of will, mastery of oneself is presupposed. If we would really dominate others it is indispensable that we gain the mastery over ourselves; and to arrive at this end we should begin by defining the nature of this force, so superior to others that make more noise but lack its solid value.

Self-mastery is a quality of the will that permits us to choose with reflection the act that we wish to accomplish. It is the power of directing its proper actions to their rightful aim, while at the same time freeing them from all foreign preoccupations. More than this, it is above all that which gives us the power to rid ourselves of foreign suggestions.

By the word "foreign" we further mean the conquering of other than the motives opposed to the resolution we have fixt upon. The domination that one submits to nearly always has its source in the egoism of our neighbour, whose views are different from ours. It is a rare thing when egoism is not paramount as the vital sentiment, urging upon others those things which are to our advantage. Rarely do counsellors yield to an impulse devoid of the element of personality: it is always in their own interest, tho sometimes unconsciously, that they seek to impose their will upon others.

There are certain persons who know so well how to set off their insinuations that they present them without showing any particular interest, dwelling merely on the least, but all the while directing them toward the path that seems most propitious for the accomplishments of the secret desire.

Now the man without power of will, his very existence depending on the will of others, is glad to find in the latter that pretext for decision which he finds wanting in himself.

Supposing that the givers of advice are clever and dishonest; persons without strength of character will be no more in their hands than so many jumping-jacks, of which their intriguers pull the strings making their plaything perform easily the acts that they can not or dare not perform themselves.

Foreign suggestions do not always come from without. They are sometimes inspired by divergent thoughts which, starting out from the subject that we are studying, gradually get so far away from them that we have to make a considerable effort of thought to get back to the genesis of their formation. Now feeble minds are incapable of this effort, and they yield to the consideration of ideas at first parasitical, then alien, whose sloping road leads them to a *terrain* that they had no intention of treading. Such persons are like those who, having set out to follow the course of a river, allow themselves, for lack of direction, to be led into adjacent canals and, from inertia and lack of resolution, allow themselves to drift along careless of the consequence.

It happens, perchance, that the excursions are not lacking in charm, that this vagabondage confined by two changing shores may not be devoid of momentary pleasures; but when it should be time to reach the destination there is no port in sight, and the eye searches for it in vain.

This negative result is always the one reached by the weak, who allow themselves to be drawn on by ideas incompatible with those to which they naturally should have recourse.

The worst of it is that these thoughts, always determining acts and not being sufficiently developed, are generally tainted with incoherence. Reason made to rule over acts and lacking a *terrain* propitious for its development, there results from this insufficiency a propensity to do certain things the effects of which can not be foreseen. In this state of things there is reason to be thankful if the resolution, due entirely to the impulse of the moment, does not come to convert these acts into irreparable errors.

All such catastrophes can be avoided by the man who knows how to govern himself.

Such a one enlarges life by opposing to adverse events that strength which is resident in himself, and which constitutes an element powerful enough to make the struggle, at first an equal one, finally yield in his favour.

The phrase "the struggle for life" has been abused, modernists using the neologism to baptize those who put it into practise "stragglers for life." There is no need of translating the term, since all the world understands it to mean the fight that is going on for existence. Unfortunately, this is not a metaphor; it may be admitted in its literal sense. The struggle that is going on between man and matter is a real one. From prehistoric times, when our remote ancestors had to combat the elements and the beasts of primeval forests, we have changed in appearance, not in reality. The end pursued by each for the purpose of conserving his own and his family's existence—what is it but the daily prey of old? It no longer takes the form of a combat with a wild beast, but appears to us in the aspect of a hundred things essential to life, things that our activity and cleverness must overcome. The motives and the aims which animate the peaceable employee in an office are the same as those which haunted the dark thoughts of prehistoric man.

To assure oneself the means of living and of embellishing life—this is the aim of all of a man's acts. Life is a struggle; but a harmonious life of the noble type is a triumph.

Consider the successful, who, urged on in the attainment of their goal, hardly turn aside to count the victims they abandon in their path. Perhaps this indifference will be branded by strict morality, but it must be kept in mind that the victims are always the feeble, those who could not fight, and lacked even the energy to steer clear of a course too dangerous for their weak equipment.

Not to be of the weak; that is the all-important thing, all is summed up in it. Man must tend toward perfection. To surpass himself will always be the objective of the man who has not been satiated by the triumph of a day.

All great inventions have made victims.

All institutions have their martyrology; the social mechanism wills it so. There is not a single discovery whose mighty results have not been accomplished by individual misfortunes.

Things really great stand on a plane above these contingencies.

Man must follow this model: He ought himself to be good, and his motives, as well as the end which he has in view, ought to be worthy ones. Too often good and evil intermingle in the achieved result, and at times it is difficult to differentiate between them. This is why character is indispensable to the man who would succeed. He will take every means to acquire it and to augment the sum of energy at its disposal. He will force himself to distinguish the means he employs, and to contemn unworthy ones. Finally, in cultivating self-mastery he will succeed not only in attaining to it, but it will radiate from him till it reaches those who surround him and even distant things, all of which he will know how to turn to his own interest and make part of his triumphal train.

2

Calmness in Strength

Man is not always master of his feelings; that is to say, it does not always depend upon himself whether or not the solution of a given problem shall rest upon reason alone. But he is master of his acts, or, rather, he will be master of his acts from the moment he determines not to conclude upon anything until the element of character intervenes to dictate his decision. One can hardly prevent himself from having feelings; but if such belong to those classed as blamable, the law that should govern him who aims at self-control is this: Do not do that act which you are called upon the justify.

Actions are only the sanction of an emotion that seeks to affirm itself.

Persons of frail character are not sufficiently impregnated with this principle. Powerless to unravel the chaos of sensations, they allow themselves to become entangled in their mazes, merely emphasizing such acts as illustrate them and render their suppression more difficult.

It is always difficult, and at times impossible, not to yield to those feelings which have become a sort of habit of the soul; but each one can suppress their manifestation, especially if they clash with the laws of common sense and morality.

Supposing you are a miser, you can not escape a disagreeable impression at the sight of money being spent; but this propensity, examined calmly and represt by the reasonableness which comes from strength of character, becomes a simple trait of wise economy.

There is not one passion which may not, under the influence of a salutary wish, divest itself of its blamable features, and take in a certain quality of sentiment.

"The passions, for the most part," as has been said elsewhere, "take root in a sentiment worthy of praise. There is a passion which, like evil in the fable, spreads terror everywhere, and which the people in their picturesque language call a pest; it is envy, the result of moral suffering, which, pushed to the point of paroxysm, produces psychical conditions bordering on aberration. None the less, if we go back to the genesis of this leprosy of the soul, we shall find a sentiment quite noble, namely, emulation, which is born of the desire to become the equal of those who have distinguished themselves in some branch of science, or won applause by their success."

And further on, the theme is pursued:

"Take prodigality, an extremely dissolute passion. Never has a prodigal known success. Abundant harvests will never be his, for, according to the familiar saying, 'He eats his wheat from the stalk.' Reapingtime comes, but no one ever finds in the prodigal's field more than an ear or two of corn, left from the wastage of the harvest. Now this vice is nothing more nor less than the amplification of something that one can not admire enough; it is the exaggeration of unreasonable generosity which produces the spendthrift."

It is thus apparent that precious qualities can be changed into reprehensible passions, and that it is possible to mold faults into solid virtues—if only we know how to develop the necessary force of character. And one of the indispensable conditions for maintaining the *milieu* from which character must spring is calmness, without which no serious resolution can be worked out.

It is not in the heat of enthusiasm that ideas are fertilized. Unreasonable enthusiasm is generally sterile, since it always strikes a note that it can not maintain. It is impossible to prolong an infatuation, and still more difficult to exploit it with unflagging ardor. There are many reasons for this; first of all, the satiety produced by habit, which, by attenuating emotion, does not permit us to exteriorize it with uniform intensity; little by little repetition comes to annul it, rendering its manifestation painful and soon impossible. Thus, it often happens that an idea adopted with excessive fervor may be dropt before our enthusiasm and quick-succeeding satiety have permitted us to give it the consideration it merits.

Another reason is the levity with which so many adopt a proposition, governed entirely by the excitement of the moment of its conception. They plunge forward without looking ahead, and are halted by the first obstacles, repulsed and disenchanted. If necessity forces them to persevere, it is with bad grace that they set themselves to the task, without any of the necessary conditions of success, all having been sacrificed to their stupidity. Finally, it is difficult for enthusiasts to detach their attention from diverse objects of which they perceive only the attractive sides; and the infatuation that takes possession of them at sight of a new idea always has the effect of attenuating that caused by the preceding idea. From this scattering of energy must result merely efforts without appreciable result, and the too-eager aspirant, if lucky enough to escape defeat, is condemned to a kind of half-success.

How much more enviable are those who submit to the law of calmness, which permits of singleness of purpose, and may be classified as a proof of strength. Calmness, in this sense, is a state of quietude which enables us to reassemble our divergent thoughts and meditate with profit. It is always the index of power. For, while debility and stupidity squander their strength in sterile demonstrations, calmness engenders contemplation which gives to ideas of promise an opportunity to take form and develop.

Without calmness, strength of character could never exist. Calmness is a faculty which fights sentiment with sentiment. It is the mobilizing of energy, and its concentration upon the point which seems to us the most worthy of consideration. It is a sort of crystalization of passion into an intense desire to come to grips with that which seems most promising of results. It is by calmness alone that we can acquire freedom of mind, the root of unity of action which permits of activity, coordinate and complete.

Calmness is not the foe of the feelings; it is their regulator. Thanks to it, resolutions made outside the domain of caprice are not at the mercy of fancy's every wind. Calmness is a power, since it rejects all emotion, all excitation, which might prove an obstacle to clear and enlightened reflection. It releases us from the vassalage of fugitive impressions, and enables us to rid ourselves of all except the desired object.

Who has not smiled at the sight of a poodle raging at a huge mastiff? The pug attacks the Molossian from all sides—makes desperate leaps at his head, gnaws at his legs, barking furiously. The big dog contents himself with lifting his snout out of the reach of the cur's attacks, and, undisturbed by the latter's howls, would turn aside to avoid him; but this being impossible by reason of the annoyer's importunity, a mighty paw is at length lifted over the cur's fragile frame, and the ridiculous adversary takes to flight howling, giving in at the first blow in a struggle that promised to be a furious one.

For those who like to make deductions from things, and to look upon the humblest events as lessons, there is much to learn from this simple incident. When one knows he is strong he will not waste his strength in useless actions. He will let his adversary exhaust himself in ludicrous assaults, reflecting the while upon the definitive act which will put an end to the contest.

Calmness is the appanage of energy; it is the attitude of those who, conscious of their strength, have no desire to squander it in sterile efforts to prove its existence to themselves. It is impossible to attain to strength of character unless one, at the same time, enforces himself to calmness, which is the generator of the active resolution, the fulcrum of achievement.

"A dullard," says an Arabian philosopher, "once carelessly set his house on fire, whereupon by his frantic efforts to extinguish the flames he made the fire spread the more."

"The wise man will take all necessary precautions against fire, but if it breaks out, instead of precipitating himself into the midst of it with hasty, futile efforts, he will call calmness to his aid, and it will suggest to him the means to employ. When he has fixt on these he will employ them without so much as a useless gesture, and to such good effect that the time given to calm reflection will be made up a hundredfold by the coherence and appropriateness of the acts suggested."

The moral of this apolog may be applied to all the acts of life. It is a question of putting a bridle upon imprudence, and of calling to our aid in grave circumstances calm self-possession, thus bringing about the solution which never will suggest itself to a mind in the effervescence of emotion.

We can not repeat this often enough; calmness is the sign of strength, an element of victory. And what finer victory can be hoped for than a triumph over passions which belittle us and deprive us of the means of success?

The struggle is not presented to all under the same aspect. Certain vehement spirits find it harder to attain to calmness than do more apathetic ones. And in this connection we can not put sufficient emphasis upon the difference between calmness and apathy.

Superficial persons have a too-pronounced tendency to confound the two states. Calmness does not exclude energy; far from that, it often represents it. It is the mark of real strength. It is also the characteristic sign of self-mastery. Without calmness strength of character can not be really manifested, since it is calmness alone which exercises rule over virile resolutions. It is sometimes said that calmness is, above all, a mark of resignation. Sometimes it involves a condition of things which doubles the power of action. In whatever phase, calmness is a state of mind, willed and chosen.

Apathy, on the contrary, is a kind of involuntary negligence; we do not hanker for it, but we submit to it. The apathetic are those whose sensations are seldom manifested; their Bufferings, like their joys, are of an attenuated sort, or, at least, seem so; for the apathetic are sometimes simply the lazy. These last suffer as much as the sensitive, but their hate of all exertion prevents them from getting any relief in their suffering. They prefer to bear it in its entirety rather than risk the effort that might ameliorate it. The power of character will ever remain unknown to them, and all their life long they will be the plaything of circumstances which they will never have the willpower to control.

We see what an abyss separates apathy from calmness; the first depresses, the second brings comfort.

Calmness it is which permits reason to dictate decisions of importance, and, thanks to calmness, strength of character may reach development and extend its influence to each one of our acts.

In the course of this work we shall speak of the means of attaining to this precious trait of character—a trait which permits us to be masters of ourselves, so that we may read ourselves like an open book.

"Know thyself," says the sage. And we may add: "Cultivate calmness of mind, which will provide the field for putting this knowledge to profit."

3

Physical Pain and the Power of Character

By reason of its invincible robustness character is able to exert an influence of the happiest, surest kind upon physical sensations. Between the mind and the body there exists an incontestable solidarity which subjects the latter to the environment determined by the moral state. We will not enlarge upon the correlation of moral impressions and physical sensations.

Every one knows that imaginary maladies are found, not only among victims of hyperneurosis, but also among many people of sane mind whose only fault it is to give free rein to their imagination upon the appearance of the slightest illness. There is then produced a sort of suggestion which passes from the brain to the part affected, the least symptoms of pain being thus heightened.

An old physician once said to a young woman who was complaining of various troubles for which she asked of him a remedy: “Don’t think of them; it is the most powerful of all cures.”

The two active elements, physical and moral, are then so intimately intertwined that to think of pain is enough to aggravate it. There is no need, however, of referring to these trivial cases; we will consider one in which the malady is not at all a question of nervousness. We will admit that it exists really, indubitably, and is neither the work of an excited imagination, nor of weakness degenerating into mean and selfish fear. In this case there is no use in saying, like the physician: "Don't think about it any more." Such a resolve would be puerile, because of its impossibility and knowledge that it is an empty formula. Nevertheless, we have before our eyes every day the example of people who, tho suffering from a definite malady, can forget all about it when their minds are occupied by something of importance that does not allow them to dwell upon their physical condition except as a secondary consideration.

"I knew a man," relates B. Dangennes, "who was suffering from an acute form of neuralgia, which compelled him to keep in bed in a room of utter darkness during the hours the sickness was torturing him. He held that every movement aggravated the pain, and refused to make any effort. One day, when the crisis was at its height, a servant burst into the room with the news that an accident had happened to the patient's little son, who was then brought in with a broken arm. Mastered by emotion, the father got right up, sent for the doctor, and gave all necessary directions. When the arm was reset, the child comforted, and the father sought to regain his bed, it dawned upon him that during this whole time he had given hardly a thought to the suffering which had excluded everything else from his mind. Struck with amazement at the proof that painful suffering might be diminished by occupying one-self with something entirely foreign from it, he decided to start anew from that day. He made more and more effort, humored his neuralgia less, and finally felt the pain decrease and even had intervals of complete relief."

We have similar examples, on a smaller scale, before our eyes every day, and may, if we are in good faith, actually prove in our own persons the truth of this observation. It is, then, the part of wisdom to create the diversion which is supplied to us by some emotion, whose vibrations, by producing in the brain a vital movement, result in a tension foreign to that of the physical pain.

We have here the triumph of strength of character.

History is filled with examples which serve to prove that physical pain can be decreased by effort of will to divert the human mind into opposite channels. Posidonius said in the midst of sufferings caused by a grave sickness: "In order to forget my suffering, and prove my contempt for it, I find it good to discourse upon pain in general, and what I feel of it does not prevent me of speaking of it to some purpose."

Have we not all read episodes of the death of the martyrs, wherein it is told how they suffered the worst tortures with amazing serenity? How some of them, escaping death, declared that their attitude was not the pride that would foil the torturer of the joy of tasting the anguish of his victims, but was the effort of will that transported them into that heaven which they had the conviction that they would conquer for themselves. The foretaste of the vision of Paradise gave them, then, the power to conceive so strongly of the paradisiacal joys as to produce in them a moral tension the intensity of which made them forget physical torture.

Do we not, indeed, see much nearer at hand, men and women who abandon the flowery existence which might be theirs, for the joy of sacrifice? They give up their freedom, sleep on a board, eat in small quantities what would not satisfy a pauper, suffer cold, seek no surety for the future, and yet experience not the multiplied sufferings that all this would seem to portend, but a plenitude of well-being which makes them forget cold, hunger, and loss of liberty. They are animated, like the ancient martyrs, by an idea whose obsession has become a source of strength; the joys of the future which they call eternity makes the rod that leads to it seem sweet. Without, however, taking up the cult of mysticism, it is given to each one of us to lessen bodily pain by making use of some preoccupation that will have weight enough to act to advantage upon physical impressions. One hears something like this every minute without being struck with the banality of it: "If I did not have to do such or such a thing I wouldn't have got up, such is my headache."

If it be desirable to go further in this matter of evoking before the mind deductive examples of this kind, here are two: On one hand a man is lowered into his bed suffering a martyrdom which is increased by the accumulation of his thoughts, all converging upon his physical condition. He can neither read nor speak, but keeps up a continual *tete a tete* with his sickness, which is the only means of combat left to him by his cerebral inaction.

The other picture is that of a man intent in the midst of his sufferings upon the thought of the necessity of leaving his bed. This thought engenders a resolution; and, while it is taking form, he forces himself to ignore his pain which, moreover, had already begun to absorb his exclusive attention. With the decision to get up and go out comes the wish to make the necessary movements to accomplish the act. This wish gives birth to a desire to get better, which undergoes such rapid development as to suggest the power of acting, just as if he were already well. Our man, helpless and inert a moment ago, surmounts his weakness and is already at his toilet preparatory to going out. He is now in the street and his *amour propre* takes a hand; to look ill and wretched is repugnant to him; he braces up, and his preoccupation in making a good appearance diminishes the effects of his illness. Finally, the thought of the walk by degrees takes the place of the thought of his malady. To be sure, he suffers still, but this suffering has become purely physical; the brain no longer furnishes it new nourishment, and at times he forgets about it altogether. Finally, the moment arrives to accomplish the object of his setting out; his whole attention is concentrated upon the words he is to use, the arguments he is to put forward upon which will depend an acceptance or refusal, in short all the consequences of his act.

His headache has already become less racking; the truce granted to the ruling idea of suffering has done its work; this latter train of thought being diverted, moral tension canalized toward another object alters the act which is taking place in the centers of motivity, and only the throb of physical pain is felt dully by the brain. We do not here intend to enter the domain of scientific exposition, which lies beyond the range of this book, but every one knows the power of suggestion when it is applied according to the rules of rigorous research.

From all this, then, the necessary deduction is that the force that resides in character can be applied to sickness with efficacious results. We do not say that it suppresses illness, but in cases not of fatal nature it makes the patient almost forget his malady for a time, enabling him to endure its graver phases by momentarily doing away with much of the suffering.

This effort of the will is well known to actors, who make use of it on the stage to transform themselves into the character they impersonate, giving the audience the illusion of reality, altho a few moments before they may have been suffering from some violent pain. What, for instance, is more painful than a jumping-toothache? Like headache, it is an evil that leaves others smiling and skeptical. Nevertheless, it makes the sufferer incapable of dissembling. Now, I have it on the word of many actors that none of them ever felt upon the stage the agonizing pain that it produces. We are speaking, of course, of real actors, those who have felt "the sacred fire." I have known them a few minutes before their entrance to walk their dressing-room, distrait, devoting their suffering to all the demons, in despair at the thought that it is impossible for them to appear. But at the voice of the call-boy they have instantly braced up, made a desperate draught upon the forces of character, and, despising the pain which a moment before prostrated them, appeared before the audience, their faces the same as ever. And for the most part there is no need of their troubling themselves so much, for the relief so dearly wished for nearly always comes. Nevertheless, the age of miracles has gone by, and they find that the pain they got rid of while they were on the stage returns on their exit.

This is a proof, you will say, that these great manifestations of the power of character are too transitory to be really salutary. No. For the number of those who have to call upon them frequently is limited enough, while those are legion who know how to put pain to sleep by a worthier kind of preoccupation. Study is a most salutary means to employ. The savant who devotes his life to important research looks upon suffering as a negligible quantify so long as it does not interfere with his work. If it gets too hard to bear, it is still in his familiar tasks that he will seek temporary oblivion.

It is, then, indispensable for all who endure bodily pain that they call to the rescue the strength that comes of character, and this will enable them to weigh the means of opposing this enemy of a redoubtable adversary, whether under the form of a desired object, a responsibility, or some wished-for ideal. It is the force of character proceeding from a strong desire for realization which, by giving their life a motive foreign to the pre-occupation caused by their illness, endows them with the power of resisting its debilitating incitements. This strength of character, however, should inspire in them an equal moderation. It is never confined to obstinacy in the connection that we have been speaking about. There is more real energy in the application of prudence than in that excess which is too often due to ultra-nervousness. For the latter strength is often indispensable. There are miseries of a physiological nature which only an operation can cure, but those of weak character can not make up their minds to undergo one. They postpone it, putting up with suffering that poisons their life, and recoiling like cowards from the necessary remedy. They thus drag out a miserable existence, lacking the strength of character which would free them from the suffering that they have not the strength to struggle with successfully.

Does this mean that it behooves us to practise the stoic doctrine in its pristine purity? Other times other manners. We are too habituated to a life of well-being to follow with ease the example left us by the great dead. But even if we tried this, would we not be striking a note in the harmonious ensemble that success demands. In fine, it is important, above all, to regard the stoic wisdom as the resultant of a spirit of resignation not easily admitted by our age.

Men of the present day should be combative; it is from this point of view that it is essential that they measure their strength with physical pain, but by showing it they give proof of inferiority. We are no longer annihilated by society, but are become part of its active machinery.

Resignation, to be sure, is a very worthy form of strength of character, but it must only intervene after accomplishment. It is only when one is convinced of the futility of his acts that he should resign himself to submit to what it is beyond his power to avoid. But up to the moment when this has been proved one should struggle by every means that strength of character suggests against the invasion of any evil whose increasing would mean our diminution.

4

Opposing the Assaults of Destiny

Every human being is responsible for his own development, is the architect of his own up-building. That is to say, it is the duty of each one to make a thorough inquiry into the sentiments that master him, and he must rely upon his strength of character to alter or modify them in the way that seems most profitable for his self-improvement. Various tendencies may have upon determinations a directing influence which will incline them to this side or that. It is only by virtue of strength of character that harmony will come to dominate. This faculty, moreover, is susceptible of dissimilar applications according to the nature of the impressions it brings out or suppresses. It supposes, then, natural feelings as well as conditional or contrary feelings, according to the nature of that which it is a question of encouraging or destroying.

What we call destiny is usually nothing more than the ensemble of facts provoked by our attitude toward events. To believe that destiny is something immovable, something inscribed, as it were, in the book of fate, would be to discourage all initiative, to fetter all perseverance. It would sanction moral and physical inertia and be an incitement to belief in fatalism. In fact, if one admits that it is impossible to struggle against destiny, what good are efforts aimed at bettering things? Why arm against a catastrophe that we can not avoid? Why not remain inert when it is useless to give battle, leaving destiny to work its will.

This is a doctrine cherished by the feeble because it gives them an excuse and a pretext. It is their excuse for inaction made to those to whom they must render an account. Also it is a pretext they love to give themselves for apathy. When through their negligence the thing that they have made a vague attempt at miscarries, they never fail to make some such remark as, “Well, what can we do? This thing was not to succeed.” Or, “Fate is against me; one can not fight against destiny.” It is such principles as these that swell the ranks of the incapable and the indolent. The fact is that one must fight against destiny, and numbers of people there are who know how to conquer it. The hostile forces that so many persons pretend environ them simply emanate from themselves and their feebleness. They are the instincts that will does not discipline and which lack the favorable guidance of sane reason. What would you think of him who instead of trying to build up a fortune of his own, remained inactive with the remark, “When destiny wills it I shall become rich.” The chances are that unless he is provided for destiny will decline to interest itself in such a worthless individual, and will let him die of hunger.

Destiny is ever blind and deaf, and we can not make it hear or regard us. It is cruel and unjust, and, as the saying is, knocks at random. But are we certain that we have never deserved its blows and done what is necessary to parry them? There are people whose alleged misfortunes would constitute real happiness for more sensible persons.

Every one has heard the story of the coach that broke down. Its occupant took the road for the nearest village where he inquired for a vehicle, adding that he had been forced to abandon his own because it was done for. There was a man in the inn who overheard the traveler; without saying a word he set out for the scene of the accident, found the carriage, and set to work fixing it. On the morrow he apprized the traveler that in return for a sum named he would engage to procure him a vehicle that would take him to his destination. The proposition was accepted and it was not without a good deal of surprize that the traveler found himself facing his own carriage which, by the owner's too ready discouragement, had become the property of the man who was able to put it to some use.

We are apt too often to act like this traveler when overtaken by an unforeseen misfortune. We yield to barren discouragement, while another less weak would take advantage of this event that we regard as a calamity, and lacking complete success would extract a certain measure of consolation from circumstances regarded by us irreparable.

This furnishes an example of the trait of strength of character of which we have just been speaking, the trait which develops in us the ability to combat that obscure entity which the feeble call destiny and men of character name the future.

One works out his own happiness, whatever pessimists may say. This faculty of enjoyment we carry within us, but with the feeble it remains in embryonic state, its power of expansion being limited to those imbued with sufficient strength of character to bring it to light.

Happiness is not what so many persons think it to be. The greater part of those who complain that they have never met with it represent it to themselves under the form of a sky that no cloud has ever darkened. These persons are ever ready to overwhelm with reproaches adverse fortune just as soon as the slightest thing happens to alter the inexact formula that represents it for them. Such people are like the Sybarite of antiquity who, finding nothing to reproach fate with, and *blase* on all kinds of happiness, complained of being wounded by the petals of roses which strewed his couch.

No, happiness does not reside in a succession of great joys ending in enthusiasm. Considered thus, it becomes a Utopia, the impossibility of its realization being the punishment of those who have had the weakness to believe in it. Happiness is within us; it surrounds us; it lies in grateful harmony, in the comprehension of the of nature; it is made of the admiration that we feel at the sight of a beautiful sunset, of the satisfaction we have in hearing a fine musical composition. In a more prosaic way we find it in family life, in the sweetness of friendship, in the pride of success achieved after long effort.

For certain of the elect it resides in the conception of personal value and in consciousness of progress toward self-perfection. For the savant it lies in discovery, and even in the researches that lead to the desired result. For all, in fine, it consists not in things of imposing character but in a series of humble satisfactions the sum of which is enough to counterbalance the inevitable boredom of existence.

We are here referring to habitual conditions only; we have not taken account of great catastrophes such as wreck lives, leaving nothing but debris after them. But even in the latter case it must not be forgotten that we can rebuild on the ruins; and indeed, for the most part, it is out of the crumbled material of demolition that new buildings are often constructed.

This is not addrest to persons of feeble character, who are prone to sit and weep amid ruins. Such as these are likely to go a long time without shelter. I am speaking to the strong, to those of virile character who win never admit defeat and lose no time in weeping; these have something better to do—to act; misfortune with them is belittled; soon it is forgotten; or eventually is transformed by them into prosperity. Even if circumstances do not permit them to reconstruct their initial success, they never consume themselves in foolish regrets, but make the best possible use of the new conditions. They will force themselves to forget the bad features of the situation, and extract from it only the good.

"I never knew the delights of walking," remarked a man of this sort of character, "until after I was ruined. Formerly I always used to ride, and never had a chance to enjoy the beauties of the road; now I go on foot, wondering at everything that I used hardly notice, and thankful for the misfortune that has given me so many little pleasures hitherto unsuspected."

Happiness, as conceived by a great many people, can not help becoming monotonous in time. Is not boredom well represented in a person having the means of instantly gratifying every possible desire? It is the delight of strong characters to conquer by a straggle the things they covet Having longed for them, they set their whole will to obtaining them. How precious now is their possession!

Such as these never became *blase,* since the bent of their character, whose strength incites them to militant labor, always tends to the attainment of a new goal, the preceding one having been reached. Those who know how to will and act rarely become the playthings of destiny; they have the world for a stage whereon to exercise their faculties, and food for interest is never lacking. With such persons resignation is not a habitual trait—far from it. Resignation accords little with force of character. It is praiseworthy only as a transient virtue. With strong men resignation is a sort of meditation; it is the homage that they render to the violence of circumstances, the recognition of their temporary supremacy. Now the very consciousness of a superior force proves strength of judgment; it can hot but produce desirable results, for it implies the resolution to adopt a line of conduct which tho unadapted for the time being will be profitable in the future, when cool judgment and organized resistance can be brought to bear. Only fools hurl themselves at an impregnable wall. Those endowed with strength of character measure with the eye the instruments needed to surmount the obstacle. The feeble, after a seeming attempt, allow themselves to sink to the ground in sterile resignation.

The word resignation is too often employed to designate the temporary acceptation of an inevitable misfortune. The strong are never willingly resigned, or at least their resignation is nothing more than an armistice during which they meditate their next attack. The apparent resignation of these is often merely the stoicism of which we have already spoken. Now we must not confound moral stoicism with stoicism in presence of physical ills. The latter is the very creditable opposing of one force to another force, against which indifference is the most potent weapon. The former consists of careful reflection with a view to attenuate the consequences, or to take measures against the act which seems about to overwhelm us. To this kind of courage is also given the name of philosophy; it is what permits us to endure adverse fortune and, at need, to return Wow for blow.

Another form of strength of character is patience. This denotes under its silent aspect a kind of energy that is not appreciated as much as it deserves to be. Patience has done more for the happiness of many a destiny than have qualities of the most brilliant type. To put it in practise is needed more strength than is required for action. Action tries the nerves, replies to a need for exteriorization from whence always results a certain solace. But that which is in expectation demands a great deal of self-mastery which strength of character alone can develop. To take part with apparent impassibility in great events effecting our interests is an effort possible only to virile souls; and to accomplish it with success the latter must be impregnated with the qualities we have described.

There is still another kind of patience in the arsenal of character which may be used against the assaults of destiny. It is that which, born of plodding perseverance, moves on obscurely but surely toward its goal, destroys one after another all obstacles, and arrives at the heart of its objective before the enemy has divined its presence.

It is the virtue of those who undertake enterprises of great range; where nervousness or haste would compromise all, they wait enduringly for the hour to show themselves and then act in good earnest. Some will say, when these succeed, that destiny has shown them partiality. But would not it be more just to give them credit for the strength of character they have availed themselves of, and to cite them as examples for the dull and impatient who, having spoiled their work by inopportune hastiness never fail to calumniate and complain of fortune's blows.

As a general principle, one should always mistrust those who complain of their lot. Destiny is cruel only to the weak who do not know how to resist its blows. It is merciful for men of strong will who brave it face to face and compel it to mercy by the power of character, engendering by turn energetic resolves and patient maneuvers, expectant action, and militant initiative; add to this a certain assumption of weakness—a formidable weapon, showing itself in the guise of a temporary inertia suddenly transformed into deeds of courage and intelligence.

5

The Struggle Against Enfeebling Sentiment

The sentiment that strength of character has most frequent need of exerting itself against is love in all its forms. This sentiment, when conceived by strong natures and addrest to those worthy of comprehending it, can become an unrivaled comforter.

Maternal love in its highest expression is the lever that can remove numberless obstacles; it is also the *viaticum* that enables children to set out bravely upon life's journey. The love of parents for their children, accordingly as it is impregnated or not with the enlightened firmness that comes of strength of character, may be for them a safeguard or a baleful gift. Many parents imagine that they fail in their duty unless they show their children an indulgence which sometimes degenerates into culpable weakness. This kind of indulgence, it is well to realize, is rarely due to fine feeling. It generally answers to a narrow egotism, which yields to the child the thing it desires when it would be wiser to refuse it. The most common cause of the spoiling of children, as it is called, is a certain thoughtless selfishness which makes the mother dread the little one's crying, as something disagreeable. She yields to the child on the plea of love and goodness, being unable to refuse it anything. How much more intelligent is the love of those parents who can resist a storm of tears and are able to make the child understand the reasons for refusing its wish. If the child is too young to reason with, the parent's strength of character will none the less make its influence felt and the baby mind will perceive the first gleam of the idea of duty. Later on, virile qualities will show themselves in such children and impel them in the right direction.

Another debilitating kind of sentimentality relates to the question of separation. Many parents prefer to see their children vegetate near them, rather than have the satisfaction of knowing that they are happy and prosperous at a distance. Such blind affection gives rise to sentiments that are most debilitating. Nothing encourages in children such mental flabbiness as the attempt to spare them all responsibility. The strong men are those who could not be held in the maternal nest after they had reached the boundary of childhood, and whose parents had admonished them early of life and its responsibilities.

Does this mean that the children should quit their parents and take flight like the birds of the air as soon as their wings are fledged? Nothing is farther from our desire than to do anything to sap the wonderful institution of the family. But in order that this institution should conserve all its value and attractiveness it should always be a haven, never a prison. The home loses its charms just as soon as these become obligatory; constraint has never yet welded souls; while a gentle firmness joined to an ample range of ideas implying a wise freedom of conduct result in that mutual understanding without which any association based on affection can not exist.

It is the same with friendship. This perfect union of hearts and minds abhors affectation as much as it does obstinacy. Friendship does not mean an exclusive reciprocal sentiment. It consists in that fulness of devotion to which strength of character sometimes gives the stamp of sacrifice. Friendship is never perfect until it is denuded of petty incidents which, far from augmenting it, impart to it the character of a selfish passion. When addrest to a person of the weak type it can become positively atrophied, with the result of producing a kind of moral fragility; for if a strong soul is frequently seen to communicate its virility, it is not a rare thing to recognize degeneracy in him who binds him-self by ties of friendship to one of feeble character whose inclinations he is powerless to guide. Nothing is more contagious than softness and inconsistency. This may be accepted as a rule without exception. When two human beings help each other by a mutual interchange of moral qualities, the resulting friendship will form their characters and make them blend. The stronger intellectually must then make an effort to fashion his friend in his own image; if not, he will find himself becoming the reflection of the other.

There is another sentiment which, when shared by noble minds, can become the ornament of life. Love does not comport with ignoble minds, for if it did it would straightway take its place among the unavowable passions. It must show itself, after a noble fashion, without any hint of prudery, a thing which always denotes a subjection to sensual motives. The giving of oneself should always be the seal of the union of two souls who are impelled toward moral beauty, encouraged by a certain loftiness of character which will preserve them from all that soiling contact so menacing to the poorest of sentiments.

To the married, strength of character is indispensable, since it enables them to tolerate without bitterness each other's mutual frailties. Perfection is not of this world, and it is difficult to exact it when one thinks how far he is from possessing it himself.

Patience, indulgence, of which we have just been speaking, are therefore virtues worth cultivating if we are to live a harmonious life.

There remain circumstances in which strength of character may intervene successfully. In the first place, we must give consideration to the impulses that a fleeting sentiment may set in motion. People of weak character yield readily to the solicitation of the moment. The flutter of sense is something they can not resist. They have not learned to make distinction between the race-instinct and the emotions whose principle rests in the attaining to a higher evolution. Character bulwarks the directing idea of all sentiment, striking its roots in aspirations which are beyond the reach of physiological considerations. Gross appetites are merely the portion of those whose brittleness of character makes it impossible for them to maintain themselves in the higher regions where self-mastery is supreme. By opposing our too-instinctive desires by strength of mind we can prevent their undue extension; especially can we effect this by trying to alter their course in making them blend in the noble enthusiasm of some great idea. This is the way to keep from pitfalls, which we look back upon with astonishment, so easily might they have been avoided.

It is profitable to associate this powerful sentiment with the diverse elements of personality as well as with the qualities of the object itself, to the end that we may blend what there is of instinct into a harmonious whole based on the sympathy of souls. The vertigoes, the excesses, the debasement caused by passional emotions ill-represt may all be avoided by him who has made it a law always to oppose the impulse of nascent passion by the power of reason.

Fragile sentimentality has still another regrettable result, it tends to skepticism. Successive disillusions always engender a penchant for doubt, that destroyer of self-confidence. Those are rare in number who will confess that their self-deceptions are due to the characteristic trait, which is speedily determined by constant obedience to instinct. Instead of yielding to the thorough self-examination of conscience, dictated by strength of character, they prefer to indict the inconstancy of others, summing up in their condemnation the whole sex whom they hold responsible for their suffering. A serious reliance upon themselves, through meditation, would quickly show them the emptiness of their recriminations. They would recognize that their light-mindedness, their enslavement to physical emotion, are the main causes of the disenchantment which leaves them broken. They will be convinced of the emptiness of ignoble passion and will make the firm resolution never again to engage the heart without the soul. Even in this last case, however, it may be admitted that sentimental error is not included and may become the source of grievous suffering. But those who have strong character will be enabled to find in a diversion strongly willed, a means of consolation for evils which in time will diminish to the point that it will require an effort of memory to resuscitate the old sorrow, now buried under preoccupations calm and sane. They can thus congratulate themselves on having by manly effort escaped the thrall of debilitating sentiments, a sort of tyranny that reason and conscience alike disallow.

There are still other passions which, if not restrained by firmness of mind, take the shape of an invading host, marring and usurping the realm of character and preventing its development. They begin, for the most part, by tendencies that thrive on moral atony, becoming in time dangerous. It is soon time to tear them up by the roots, but indolence does not permit the necessary effort and we quietly allow them to grow into defects of which we become the slaves. It has now become impossible to escape their exigencies. Self-mastery neglected revenges itself, and the vassalage of ignoble ideas asserts its rule over the non-resistant. In each individual there are a number of "egos" which often find themselves in opposition. Now for insufficiently nourished souls nothing is more weakening than internal conflict. What must be done is to supplant one desire by another, one appetite by another appetite.

What means has any one of seeing clearly into himself unless strength of character supervenes to impose its logic and direction? Those who do not know how to summon their aids in the hour of trouble are like the bird that dashes himself against the wires of his cage, seeking an outlet that does not exist till some one opens the door.

Strength of character is the bay opening upon the seas of moral liberty—and material liberty too, we may add—for mastery of self engenders success whence flows independence. Mental strength, then, not only is the cause of moral liberty but is also a means of acquiring individual liberty.

Perhaps we have already used up too much ink in establishing the parallel between individual restraint and social restraint to linger any longer upon the subject. None the less we must insist upon this point; moral liberty engenders individual liberty whence proceeds, in a certain measure, social liberty. We say in a certain measure, for no civilized human being can disengage himself from his duties to his kind. These obligations, however, may be agreeable and comforting, provided that they are performed freely and by personal choice. Binding in their nature, they should rarely be of the instinctive sort.

All designs looking to the betterment of others should be guided by reason. To act without consulting it would mean yielding to acts of impulse, especially to egotism, which, in the absence of reflection, dictates all human actions. This would be to bring upon the scene vanity and stupidity, whose consequences go on multiplying by the piling up of the errors they involve. Goodness without strength of character is a feeble virtue, working at random and at the hazard of momentary fancy. Those, moreover, who practise it, if they are honest, admit to themselves the inferiority of their motives. Unreasonable goodness is often nothing more than sensibility based on egotism. We relieve another's suffering so that he will stop bothering us, altho our motive never appears to us in the brutal form in which we here depict it There are, in fact, very few persons capable of thus analyzing their intentions. It is apparent in this connection that, if the suffering were felt by some unknown person, and did not touch us, we would be in no hurry to go to the rescue.

There is in small charitable manifestations an unconscious egotism which we translate by pity, a sentiment that comes of our satisfaction at having escaped the suffering we relieve. The goodness which is tempered by strength of character knows nothing of these transactions, ignored by ourselves but thoroughly debilitating in their effect. It acts without evoking the personal element to the slightest extent. It will sometimes take on the aspect of insensibility, but the feelings it elicits are always of lasting quality, and its motives, being of the higher order, give to its realizations a largeness of range unknown to the common type of goodness, which acts without knowing whether it tends or what may be its results.

Pity, when it does not possess equality and aim at rehabilitation, may also be classed among the debilitating sentiments. It may be acquired by the cultivation of reason. The idea of protection, unless it involves aspiration toward equality, always has a lessening effect upon its object Sentimentality is the last consideration for him who wishes to take character for his guide. Does this mean that he must be hard-hearted and without feeling? The best way to answer this question is by asking another. Are those who make a display of sentiment, themselves exempt from selfishness? And since this is the trait that is the most common, and that which stamps nearly all, why not make of it a source of strength instead of allowing ourselves to be shackled by it? Why not transform an obstacle into a weapon of defense?

Reasonable egoism may be more fruitful of pity, when freely avowed and directed toward a noble object, than when it is disguised in the traits of banal goodness, whose manifestations, always ephemeral and insufficient, belittle the one to whom they are addrest in emphasizing his inferiority and dependence.

6

Fear and Strength of Character

One can not help pitying, while also slightly despising, those whom lack of willpower renders slaves to that tormenting weakness, fear.

Fear is a kind of shadow constantly hovering over life, for it has no need of reason for its existence. It shows itself in everything, poisoning moments the most delightful, spoiling the most legitimate pleasures. Fear is a sort of anguish caused by a danger, real or imaginary, and seems to involve powerlessness to will anything except retreat. Usually it has no reason for its existence, since it is far from furnishing a solution of any kind. True, in most cases, the object of terror being undefined, retreat is an instinctive resort; it means escaping some unknown danger, the presence of which nothing suggests. At times fear is of partly unconscious nature, participating in the instinct of conservation. The sensitive feel it at the slightest approach of danger. It is almost impossible to conquer it without having resort to strength of character, for reasoning has no effect upon persons prone to fear.

Every one tries to convince nervous people of the harmlessness of thunder. Nearly every one knows that the danger is past when the clap of thunder is heard. Nevertheless, in spite of all scientific proof, in spite of their own inward conviction, they tremble with apprehension after the flash of lightning, holding their ears in the most childish fashion.

Others have an invincible fear of darkness. They know perfectly well there is nothing in the darkness, but they would not venture into it for the whole world. For them deprivation of light constitutes actual suffering; they people the obscurity with a fantastic world of menacing larvae and fantoms.

Those who are afflicted with this weakness can not cultivate too earnestly strength of character, which will give them prohibition against a return of their agonizing terrors.

For their fear is caused by nothing else than weakness. This is the necessary deduction of all who have ever been among the timorous. The slightest company, no matter if it be some weaker than themselves, reassures them. They do not reflect that in case of attack their companion will be more embarrassment than aid; for the proper trait of fear is not to reflect at all. If persons given to fear took the trouble to think, they would perceive that their defect has a contemptible foundation; mistrust of their own merits and an exaggerated idea of weakness, which can be reassured by the presence of a child. If they kept their ideas clear they would see that such company, instead of an advantage, would be an additional reason for disquiet. For if there were any real danger, it would be their duty to protect the child, who would thus add to the complications. We do not admit that they might think of abandoning it, but if such an idea should occur to them it would furnish one example the more to show to what lengths fear will go in annihilating all moral sense. Their painful anxiety over, and sane reason reinstated, they are likely to blunt at themselves for their conduct, and this will be a step in the right direction.

Numbers of people imagine they exculpate themselves by the excuse, "I lost my head for the moment." This excuse aggravates the matter, for to lose one's head is the most blamable of all weaknesses. One could hardly pardon a child for resorting to this pretext, but in an adult it is the *cachet* of impotence as well as the confession of defeat.

Fear, like many maladies, is particularly contagious; it is communicated to children in stories told by nurses who, especially if unenlightened, risk poisoning the lives of their charges and those belonging to them. For cowards like to make converts; it seems that their defect takes on a less shameful aspect the more it is diffused, and they love to sprcad the contagion among those that surround them.

For this weakness there is only one remedy—strength of character, which will maintain the willpower sufficient for the struggle. It is usually more than useless to reason with the timorous, especially at the critical moment, their reply to all arguments being, "I am afraid." The simplest way is not to try to convince them they are wrong in yielding to fear, but to supply them with the means of mastering their weakness. One way is to send the timid one into a darkened room for something, having convinced him that there is nothing there to fear. Only on his return should recourse be had to the language of reason. Let the first attempt at treatment be simply an order.

The timid are nearly always obedient; their nature leaves them open to impression by a superior will, and fear of the complications involved in rebellion induces them to overcome their defect. The first victory ought immediately to be followed up by a second one. To accustom the patient to darkness should be one of the first cares in the reforming of a timid nature. He should be accompanied at first and got used to it, and the conversation should avoid all disquieting subjects.

It is to be noted, further, that those given to cowardice are prone to recall those things that frighten them. With teeth chattering they will talk of ghosts and apparitions, and it is difficult to awaken in their minds the recollection of subjects other than terrifying. Setting apart this unhealthy propensity to seek after sensations of fanciful nature, which recall certain maniacs who take pleasure in aggravating a wound, this habit must be ascribed to the unique preoccupation that haunts their brain in the darkness. This is why it is necessary to give their thoughts a different direction. And, later on, when they are sent into the dark alone for a few minutes, care must be taken to demand of them something requiring them to reflect a little before answering, the response to be deferred till their return from their little adventure.

Fear does not resist the power of derogatory thoughts, and he who can conquer sufficient strength of character to bring about this resistance is very near to a victory over this hideous defect which is so fatal to the sufferer.

Still another source of fear that moral strength may come to sap to some extent is the tendency to superstitious beliefs, which deform the mind by substituting for judgment some absurd belief repulsive to reason. There exist perfect skeptics in religious matters who turn pale as they see a crow flying on their left. Others will never undertake anything on Friday. Still others there are who would not for the whole world take a decisive step on Friday, should it fall on the thirteenth of the month. Certain men, otherwise intelligent, fill their lives with these superstitions, with the result that their intellectual faculties become tainted. It is only by force of character that they can free themselves from such enslavement.

These, just like the victims of fear, should study the sources of their beliefs, and honestly acknowledge that they are based solely on traditions established by coincidences. Legends of apparitions are nothing but the result of unnatural observations. Superstitions relating to such or such encounters, or to some incident or other, are the result of some remark lightly, or perhaps designedly, made. There are none so blind as those who will not see, as the saying is; and we may add there is no worse clairvoyant than he who is bent on seeing some particular thing. Now, one imbued with a superstitious mind finds coincidents in the most ordinary circumstances. Let some pleasure come to him when he happens to be wearing a certain costume, and he will put it on again in the hope that his walk will bring the desired result. If, on the contrary, on meeting some person bad luck follows, he will try to avoid him for the future or examine into every thing that happened on the day of the meeting.

Superstition is always based upon superficial observation, and denotes feebleness of mind which should be combated by reason. To impose resistance of any value upon excessive credulity character must intervene. We must oblige ourselves to act as if we were untouched by superstition. Just as soon as it points to some act which must be avoided, that is the very thing to do, if it is not something wrong. On the other hand, we must be on our guard against what the arbitrary creed prescribes. For example, some one upsets the salt cellar; instead of being in a harry to throw salt over the left shoulder (interrupting the conversation the while), lest bad luck should fall on the company, use some willpower, refrain from flinging salt over your shoulder, and take up the conversation at the point where it was halted by the accident. Then in all honesty ask yourself conscientiously what are the consequences of this abstention. When it is established that no misfortune has happened as a result of disregarding the prescribed exorcisms the inanity of the popular belief will be admitted. No real relationship being seen to exist, reason will oppose itself to a number of similar unexpected happenings. But before we can invoke reason it is urgent that we resolve to follow the counsels which flow from deductions made in cold blood and devoid of partiality.

Character, then, is indispensable in inspiring the courage essential for sane reasoning, and also for keeping the resolutions prompted by such reasoning. In the cure of fear it will intervene in the way we have described; and from the time that improvement is observable the patient should try to continue himself his education in courage.

The means most certain and that we can not insist enough upon is to substitute for thoughts of fearful nature those totally different, yet interesting enough to make an impression upon the mind, but detrimental to what it is desired to do away with. No one has ever been mastered by a violent sentiment without perceiving that the ordinary fears that assail him instantly vanish. We often hear of cowards who become paralyzed with fear in the dark, setting out in the middle of the night for a doctor without feeling any of the terrifying sensations that ordinarily assail them. The reason is that their brain, dominated by the thought of the help that must be got, the preoccupation of haste and the worry caused by the illness of some dear one, has room for no idea except the agonizing one of the moment. In presence of that all others vanish. The immediate representation does away with all others, and fear flies before an emotion stronger still.

To conquer fear, then, it suffices to have recourse to the things that contribute to make strength of character; the will to possess them. This may pass for a jest with some. They will say that if you need will in order to get possession of it "the fat's in the fire," for they acknowledge themselves to be incapable of shaping any desire with intensity.

The thing to do is not to try to conquer willpower at the first blow; it is enough to hare some valid hope of success in this direction.

This is the first step. The second consists in strengthening oneself for the attempt, and not offering any resistance to the doctrine itself.

To recognize one's weakness and have the desire for deliverance is the chief condition demanded for the development of a firm character. Meanwhile we must force ourselves to abandon all superstition and enfranchise ourselves from fear, just as we would divest ourselves of some uncomfortable, worn-out garment.

We have no time for the weaknesses of former epochs. We of the present age must all struggle with more or less ardor and also earnestness to conquer the place we covet and which often belongs to us by right. The coward is often, *vis-a-vis* of his adversaries, in the situation of a man disarmed and wishing to measure himself against an enemy equipped with shield and dagger. Against such a foe one weapon only is possible—strength of character, which permits its possessor to think, to resolve, and to act. He who has this and can adapt it to circumstances may face every hostile front. He is certain to issue from the fight victorious and regenerated.

PART-II

CHARACTER: HOW TO DEVELOP IT FOR BUSINESS AND DAILY LIFE

7

Exercises of the Intellect for Acquiring Strength of Character

Admitting that a little willpower is necessary in order to act upon the will, he who suffers from weakness of character and desires to fortify his mind should allow this comparison to sink deep in his memory:

> A gardener desiring to cultivate certain plants of precious kind, begins, before sowing the seed, by freeing the soil from the tares which are fatal to growth. As soon as the seeds have sprouted he further relieves them of all dangerous environment by tearing away all parasite growths, which, in spite of his care, continue to show themselves and quickly hinder the blooming of the flowers, those objects of his solicitude. These freed from their invading foes are not slow to spring up and spread their leaves, choking in turn the thin grass which grows poorly in their shade.

He who wishes to obtain strength of character should, then, above all else, try to deliver his mind from the invasion of feeble thoughts. Before seeking strength he should expel every idea of weakness; this is what might be called clearing the soil. It also gives a valid answer to those who pretend that fragile wills can never be improved, since, in order to arrive at strength of character, that qualification itself is essential.

In order to will to advantage it is necessary above all to do away with the enemies of volition. Now all weakness willed is a primordial obstacle to the installation of strength of character. For one who aspires to willpower, therefore, it is essential to avoid the thoughts opposed to its manifestations.

Resistance to willing is itself a form of willing; those, therefore, who say they are too indolent to guide their desires in the direction of strength unconsciously perform an act of the will. Would it not be more worth while if this contrary force were employed in the acquisition of so essential a quality, rather than utilized against its possession? It is certain that the act of developing moral vigor sufficient to impart energetic direction demands qualities of a special order and a regimen that can not be acquired over night. But before *willing much it* is always possible to try *to will a little.* The conquest of strength of character often rises out of the debris of moral inaction, and the latter disappears just as soon as the power of volition begins to take form in the mind which has rid itself of weakness and its depressing cortege.

The first condition, then, of this evolution is an aspiration toward the mastering of oneself, and it is not without a certain amount of agitation that this desire takes shape. It is even desirable that this emotion should take place, since from the antagonism between the old and the desired state arises nearly always a resolution that may be regarded as the embryo of character.

It has often been said by the wise that the finest victory that a man can put to his credit is that which he has gained over himself.

His resolution taken, he should enter upon the struggle against excessive emotions. Having estimated their value as the result of the first impression he will make certain to attribute to them their exact significance. He will on no account delay very long over the primitive sensation. As soon as possible after the initial shock he will impose upon himself a certain moral coldness, that is to say, he will avoid giving his imagination free rein for comment and deduction. It may even be prudent to call in some idea foreign to the incident in question. All this has no other aim than the settling down of the effervescence caused by the emotion, and always perilous for the thought.

People have a sorry habit of studying consequences in a disfiguring light. Amplification does the rest, and we soon find ourselves upon the threshold of resolves which, considered in the light of the event which prompted them, become perfectly unreasonable. For example, a person of weak character hears of a relative's illness. It is a question of a widow left with a little daughter. Straightway moral debility begins its work. The person becomes excited by the usual anticipations of pessimistic natures. On receiving the news she imagines they have not told her the truth, that the relative is going to die, and the child be left in her charge. The cortege of worries and privations that will result from this augmenting of her family defiles before her imagination, and, frightened by the thought of the responsibility about to fall upon her, she loses her head, forms resolutions which she directly abandons for new ones, and ends by making a mess of it all.

On the morrow she learns that her relative is better, and her high spirits make her forget all her anxiety on the sick woman's account, her imagination having cured the patient just as it had killed her.

If she had chosen to acquire some strength of character she might have acted differently. On receiving the bad news she should have represt all thoughts tending to make things worse, and waited for more information before making a decision.

But that is impossible, you will say, since such efforts are beyond reach of weak characters. The fact is that we do not require it of them at the very first.

When a person who has not yet achieved the conquest of himself finds himself face to face with some event designed for his overthrow his sole effort should be brought to bear upon one thing: to concentrate his ideas instead of dissipating them.

To do this he should be content with registering the fact, and then he should *immediately occupy himself with something else* for fifteen minutes up to an hour. To anticipate objection to the impossibility of this, we offer advice that will be continued at some length.

For example, one may write one or two letters in advance; this is an easy diversion. It is understood that in the letters there need be no question of what we have just learned, and the more the object of our preoccupation haunts the mind the more must we contrive to banish it. Write, then, without mentioning it, as if the letter has got the start of it by an hour. We are then rid of it for the time being, and if it is something that must be communicated to our correspondent it may be imparted when the moment of excitement is past.

The object of this exercise is to collect our ideas and prevent representations from crowding in disorder in an overtaxed brain. This accomplished, and the letter or letters written, emotion will be felt to subside, and we shall be able to think to some purpose. If, however, the thought brought back to the object that caused the agitation will not attain to coordination, if one feels himself carried away by a flood of apprehensions it will be necessary to reject them all before they become preponderant, employing meanwhile the prescribed means up to the moment when it is given to us to consider dispassionately the consequences of the thing that is tormenting us.

When we have attained to silence, and only then, we shall begin to reflect. Above all it is essential to force ourselves to take an optimistic course. It is the defect of the inconsistent to see everything in dark colors. Strong souls, on the contrary, try to search out even in shameful incidents, the features that are least so, in order to supply the more easily the remedy. It is, then, necessary to view things on their least painful side, while avoiding at the same time the lure of chimerical hope—for deceptions are bad counsellors to strength. If there be question of those things that carry in their train inevitable consequences we must face them without hesitation. To palliate them or refuse to see them as they are would be weakness. It is hard to walk in the dark, and to avoid ambushes it is well to light up the road. The thing of primary importance is to mistrust the first impulse and avoid the initial period of mental confusion. This achieved, one shall have taken a long step in the acquisition of strength of character.

A vice which is common in all those of weak

character is anger. This they allow full head-way because of a momentary sense of solace that it procures for them.

Passion is never the trait of virile natures.

They know what inferiority is stamped upon those afflicted by this habit, and they try with all the power of their will not to give way to it.

Anger is not always spontaneous with the weak. It is often the resultant of the accumulation of the representations of which we were speaking a moment ago. In common parlance, anger is said to mount, and the image is a correct one, for it is only by degrees, in certain cases, that anger invades the brain. The point of departure is often nothing more than some disagreement; but a strong imagination creates motives which give rise to irritation, which in turn increases in proportion as it registers them.

We may compare this kind of anger to a fire, harmless at first; but, built up and fed with care, it becomes a conflagration.

Passion, on the contrary, is produced suddenly and is appeased as soon as the image which has caused it no longer presents itself in vivid form. In feeble minds this attenuation occurs rapidly. They are incapable of keeping the same thought intact very long, so that the object of their resentment in passing through many rapid gradations is at last effaced.

This emotion takes on a progression directly opposite to that of the other kind. While with these latter it follows an ascending gamut and for a long time maintains itself at its maximum intensity by the renewing of its motive forces, in the case of those carried away by passion there is a constant depression whose final phase is marked by an abatement as pronounced as is the agitation itself. In both cases the irritable are victims of this defect. Judgment obscured by passion supplies them with no sensible suggestions, and they have to regret all the resolutions they have made under the influence of this kind of emotion. Nothing but an energetic appeal to character can save them.

No one need laugh at the proverb which says: "When anger is in the ascendant roll the tongue seven times in the mouth before speaking." Put in this way, the advice may seem curious; none the less it contains profound wisdom. All who are seriously desirous to oppose their natural impatience by strength of character should ponder it and put it in practise, in spirit if not literally. Let the aspirant for firmness of character, upon the appearance of irritation, impose upon himself some act that will divert his attention from the annoyance in question.

A German philosopher cites the case of a man who was noticed carrying a chain which from time to time he unrolled and manipulated in silence. One day some one asked him the reason of this. "This chain," he replied smiling, "is my bridle. I am of a very irritable temperament, and anger has often made me do foolish things which I have deeply regretted. So that I have made it a rule never to obey any emotional impulse without first letting a few moments elapse. As soon as any irritating incident rouses in me the spirit of retort, of too ready desires or resolves, I deliberately count the one hundred links of my chain, thus imposing on my mind a tension wholly bent in making no mistake in my count. This to me is an invaluable diversion. During the operation my nerves calm down, the inward disturbance is appeased, and in the mirror of my mind, now clear, wise resolutions are peacefully reflected."

The philosopher has not told us any more; but we like to think that after a while the bridle was discarded and that he who conquered strength of character by such original means did not need to have recourse to it very long.

This example ought to be a lesson to all who wish to make a conquest of character. We have said before that it is wholly made up of calmness and recollection, and without being obliged to employ such an eccentric process as that just cited, it is within the power of all to have recourse to some task at the moment when excitement is at its height. And this task, which need not interfere with the ordinary course of things, may just as well be of the moral as of the material order.

For instance, no one will notice it if a person takes out his pocketbook and counts over nine or ten cards put there expressly. The act will always be excused on the ground of forgetfulness, or of some possible error that it is necessary to guard against.

Other actions seemingly as natural as this may be arranged in advance.

During the moment we are employed in executing them the thought, forcibly diverted from its course by the act that we are engaged in and the slight effort of calculation it involves, will no longer present itself under the brutal aspect that anger clothed it with; and little by little, strength of character helping, actions of an outward character will no longer be indispensable. We shall gradually find it desirable to give our thoughts the character of contemplation, and the wished-for calm will soon come.

It would be an error to suppose that weakness can be got rid of so easily.

Relapses are sometimes numerous, but if one be strong in resolution he will remark that even relapses are the stepping-stones to firmness of character. The qualities of which this is composed are the progeny of reason. They are acquired by education and belong, like so many others, to the sphere of the practical.

Thanks to a methodical plan of vigorous elaboration and properly sustained after the manner indicated, we can bring about a sure calm after a period of agitation. The conditions of this superior evolution rest upon an initiative which can be sustained by strength of character alone. It is by this trait alone that we can know the serenity which is engendered by order and unity of thought, those elements that determine unity of action which is inseparable from success.

8

Physical Exercises for Developing Strength of Character

If the postulant follows conscientiously the counsels that we have given in the preceding chapter he will find himself disposed to wage war to some advantage upon his own weaknesses, but this will not suffice to preserve him from relapses and confirm him in sane and reasonable volition. In order that these last conditions may be fulfilled the forces of his moral nature must be based upon the power that may be obtained from physical exercises.

The first thing to do is to get rid definitely of all impulsiveness; for this defect always degenerates into nervousness and then everything must be begun over again. In the battle that the weak must fight with themselves, nervousness is the most redoubtable foe, since it is an element of disorganization. A moment's nervousness may destroy the fruits of the application of days. It fetters all reflection comprising a judgment and does not even leave willpower for discussion. It bears about with it its pitiable excuse, the excuse of a man of brittle character put forth as an extenuating circumstance: “What can you expect, I was nervous at the time.” Or the still more current one, “I had to relieve my nerves.” It would be impossible to enumerate all the foolish actions to which these two terms have given illusory protection.

It is always best to proclaim aloud that this excuse is nothing but an aggravation of the fault it seeks to palliate. Commission of it is reprehensible, but to seek to explain it by nervousness is to have it thrown out of court. If the fault is a defect the sentiment that gave rise to its commission is another, and a more important one. He who invokes this pitiful defense is like one who would say: “I have done wrong because I am bad.” It is then necessary at any cost to put a halter on impulsiveness and nervousness whenever they appear.

In connection with the exercises that we have just advised and which are related to the reflective faculty, we would also suggest exercises of physical character, with a view of conquering that kind of strength of character that we name endurance.

Endurance which takes root in moral volition demands, moreover, a certain quantity of physical energy to be maintained with success. It is the foundation stone of the edifice of character. Endurance is composed of a variety of sentiments that we shall briefly analyze:

Calmness.
A certain contempt for pain.
Patience.
Perseverance.

In the beginning of this book we stated what were the benefits to be derived from calmness. We will not return to the subject; but we are going to determine the physical means of obtaining it, having already in the preceding chapter pointed out how to conquer it in a moral sense.

Calmness is the state attained to by a man in whom moral and physical equilibrium is complete. It is a priceless possession from the fact that there are few moments in our day when it is not in requisition. The slightest incidents as well as the gravest events can cause us considerable inconveniences unless we encourage them with calmness of mind. But to be successful in the effort to keep a firm balance when subjected to the agitation of some emotion we must, as an indispensable condition, have recourse to certain physical aids. The mind can not attain to real courage unless the body comes to its aid, at least during the time of novitiate. Having called calmness to our aid by the means that we prescribed in Part I of the book, and having, after the daily examination of conscience, slept the sleep that comes of a will at perfect peace, it will be well to revive the above thought and saturate ourselves with its meaning, previous to entering upon the exercises which follow:

FIRST EXERCISE

Take a piece of cardboard the size of a large sheet of paper. Cut a hole in this cardboard which will correspond in size to an ink-stain made on a piece of paper which is to be pasted to the wall.

While comfortably seated before the ink-stain take the cardboard by the lower rim between the thumb and index finger, the arm being extended well out from the body. Tour care must now be to do what follows: Look through the hole of the cardboard at the ink-stain on the paper so that the stain is exactly enclosed, nothing of the white surface appearing to the eye.

For the first few days this visual and physical tension should not exceed twenty seconds; little by little the time may be extended. But the point is to be very particular about exactness in the experiment; no speck of white must appear to the eye during the test.

SECOND EXERCISE

We are to proceed in this as in the first, but in place of a piece of cardboard take a sheet of paper, and try to make the aperture frame the ink-stain for the eye while the paper keeps its stiffness. If the paper bends, the experiment must be tried again.

THIRD EXERCISE

Fill a glass with water to a third of an inch of the brim, and hold it toward the bottom. Hold it so that it will be on a level with a line traced on the wall.

The surface of the water in the glass must be held so that its level will not deviate from the line.

Hold the glass at arm's length from the body until you begin to feel fatigue.

When this exercise is kept up for a while it Till be possible to do it without the slightest stirring of the water.

FOURTH EXERCISE

Fill the glass now to the very top and repeat the experiment.

If the water overflows, try again.

FIFTH EXERCISE

Having filled the glass to the brim, hold it up from the bottom by the thumb and fourth finger for two seconds; then move it slowly from right to left keeping its brim level with the line which it must just graze.

These exercises, which may have the look of being devised to provoke impatience, are not always crowned with success at the first attempt. And for this very reason those who apply themselves to them conscientiously and intelligently are in a fair way to conquer their nervousness, since in the course of their experiments they will have frequent occasion to fight against this defect.

Contempt for pain is in proportion to the appraisal of the pain or the importance with which imagination invests it. Is it necessary here to repeat the story of the sick man who felt himself cured while he was knocking at the physician's door?

It is an incontestable fact that pain is increased by the anxiety it provokes. Moreover, it exists in reality in most cases; but while those who cultivate strength of character lessen the force of pain by the contemptuous fashion in which they regard it, people of feeble willpower permit it such a preponderant place in their thoughts that it is impossible for them to forget it even momentarily.

Let us add that their natural wilfulness prevents them from taking up the hygienic exercises recommended by physical culture, and known to be a sovereign remedy for the physiological miseries which sap intellectual strength.

We shall not attempt a description of those exercises

whose range exceeds the limits of our book, but in a general way we may suggest the possibility of getting control over their nerves, up to the point of being able to ignore habitual sufferings on a small scale by recourse to the following exercises:

FIRST EXERCISE

In case of indisposition, headache, rheumatism, neuralgia, if the suffering is not too acute, one should resort to some diversion of intellectual nature. For instance, take up a book and read a page or two with the object of discovering some quality or some defect. Suppose goodness is the quality we fix upon, try then to find it manifested in the pages before us. Perhaps it may happen the book contains nothing but reasoning and that goodness does not figure there at all. None the less it will be noticed that the mind-tension involved in this reading directed to an object has altered the course of the suffering and deprived it of its intensity.

SECOND EXERCISE

The reading concluded, write down the gist of it and then develop it in a couple of pages.

THIRD EXERCISE

Reduce these two pages to ten lines while taking special care to condense the meat of the argument.

FOURTH EXERCISE

Then make the endeavor to reduce these ten lines to a phrase which will sum up all the observations contained in the passage.

This is addrest as much to those who are not given to intellectual occupations as to those habitually so engaged.

Apart from immediate and pressing interest the business in hand seldom has any power of distracting us from physical suffering; while the exercises we offer have a certain novelty and attractiveness which give them a better chance of success.

Under pretext of suffering we always feel an inclination to throw up our daily labor; but if we consider work from a higher point of view and something of the utmost importance there will remain no pretext whatever for neglecting it.

Patience may be obtained by putting it to the proof in the following way:

FIRST EXERCISE

Take a handful of lead ground up like grain; spread it out upon a white sheet of paper and count the grains four times in succession. If after the first attempt there is the slightest sign of impatience, the grains must be shuffled up and the count recommenced. If the same number is not obtained at each count, try it over until the identical number occurs three times in succession.

SECOND EXERCISE

Attach a watch to the wall and without moving a muscle watch the hands for a fixt time.

(At the beginning a few seconds will be sufficient.)

THIRD EXERCISE

Having preceded as prescribed above, perform certain identical motions for a fixt time.

For example, bring the thumbs together at regular intervals, for a few seconds at first.

Then do the same with the index fingers and the remaining fingers in turn.

The duration of these exercises should be increased a little each day and kept up until the slightest sign of impatience has disappeared.

Perseverance can be acquired in the same way. And in order to give the exercises some useful aim it will be well to have some good purpose in view, such as the rendering of some service, etc. But the most important consideration of all is the determination to continue the exercises. For it must not be supposed that the mastery of ourselves is to be gained in a day. It is only to be conquered by force of will and perseverance. And this last quality will find very strong encouragement from the progress that will be observed to follow upon conscientious application. The results obtained will be a valuable aid in the achievement of our favourite ambitions.

After some days of these continued daily exercises the happy assurance will be had that nervous symptoms are becoming rarer. Physical ailing will be lessened, and we shall find ourselves giving it only the amount of attention it deserves and guarding against its encroachments. What would have passed for a catastrophe a few weeks ago is now reasonably set down for a very remediable evil. Pride of self-domination will be augmented by desire for self-perfection and the satisfaction of feeling immune from all dependence on the emotions will become the most active factor in the acquisition of that strength of character in whose practise are found consolement and encouragement.

9

Strength of Character in Business

It is in truth the philosophy of another age than ours that inculcates contempt of riches.

It need not be taken for granted that we are going to make an apology for cupidity, yet we venture to assert that at the present time every one might profit by letting the thought of the great Schopenhauer sink into his mind:

"Money is a barrier against all possible evils."

Ignoring the arguments of puritans we shall explain and make some comment upon this thought of the great philosopher.

He did not say: money is the universal remedy; he denominated it a barrier.

And how exact this attribute is. Money prevents the sufferings that come of poverty. With money, we may ignore cold and hunger; while sickness can not be obviated by money, it can be considerably relieved by it. Money gives us the satisfaction of relieving others from suffering. By money one may aid in the development of nascent genius, participate in some fine achievement. It gives one the leisure to devote a part of his time to the culture of art under all its forms.

Add to this that money can provide a powerful diversion for all troubles, by permitting of distraction for the mind from the anxieties that assail it.

We are aware that pessimists will not omit to confront this argument with the famous line:

> "And ha who keeps guard at barriers of the Louvre can not protect our kings."

But at the risk of displeasing some we venture to say that it is less painful to die in a palace, surrounded by every possible comfort, than to end one's days on a pallet, where the lack of every comfort tends to increase the rigors of the last agony. With the tender care of the best physician attainable there is much less chance of our quitting this life than would be the case if we had to forego all this for lack of money. If money does not bring positive cure it always brings alleviation.

There is, then, no discussion of the subject possible. At the period we have reached it is a bad thing to be poor; and we must try to get a thorough understanding of all that we may possibly do in an honorable and legitimate way to remedy this condition of things if it exists; or, if we belong among the privileged ones who inherit wealth, we should take every means to conserve it.

Now, the conditions of life ever becoming more and more onerous, permit scarcely any one to remain inactive. Even to those who have received wealth as an inheritance idleness is a certain cause of ruin. A great fortune exacts genuine labor as a condition for efficiency of administration. And those who leave to strangers this duty do not long deserve the title of millionaire; they soon see themselves reduced to a simple competence which for their children comes to be want. These shirkers, unless they happen to have one of those rare birds, an honest manager, pay the penalty of their negligence. The individual interests of the manager always prevail over those of the master and even abstracting the factor of indelicacy from the situation, one can hardly require a man to consider the interests of his employer above his own.

This is why a rich man who wants to preserve his fortune and even increase it ought first of all to be his own business manager.

Business is the point of departure and the chief aim of every one in the world, not excepting those placed at the head of the State; since in conducting the affairs of State these latter must also occupy themselves with their own. We will not even except artists who, provided they know how to draw from their works the price they are worth, can the more easily devote to their beloved ideals the time that their happy transactions places at their disposal.

What masterpiece can be expected of him who works for so much a day for his daily expenses. The finest talent is put in the same class with a trade and must be exercised without respite. In these conditions the finest dispositions are spoiled, the soaring thought, represt by manipulation, breaks before it can realize its fine aspirations, and is caught in a rut where it remains kept down forever.

An artist whom certain purists reproached for making a traffic of his genius made answer, "It is necessary for me to be a tradesman in order to have the right to be a genius." And history is fall of facts which confirm his dictum. Are we not assured that Solon the sage paid the expenses of his trip to Egypt by selling oil and thus traveling in comfort? Or, coming nearer home, did not the great Shakespeare adopt the occupation of theatre-manager to obtain the necessary leisure to produce his dramatic masterpieces?

Business, therefore, under the multiple forms it takes is the labor intended for all. From the bottom to the top of the ladder it is necessary to amass money to apply it to some cause or other.

Money is not what the shiftless are tempted to regard it—something that exempts us from duty; it is, on the contrary, the means by which we may fulfil them in a larger, better way. Every one, then, should in his own way and at a certain time make an effort to amass some money.

Some there are who apply money to their daily wants. Others seek it to swell the fortune they desire to leave to their children. Those still only desire it to devote it to some noble enterprise, the exiguity of their resources not permitting them to manage it in person. Finally, a large number see in it chiefly a means of immediate gratification; but all, including those who hold positions whether in the liberal professions or in the commercial world—artists, artizans, proprietors, all who are capable of earning ready money may have their work classed under the denomination of business.

A business, in whatever category it belongs,

demands for success many qualities, among which strength of character takes first rank. This latter is a weapon of defense against the worst temptations. It gives its skilful possessor a superiority over his opponents that is incontestable. Strength of character, destined to triumph in the kingdom of business, is composed of special qualities, chief of which is coolness of temperament, which proceeds from self-possession. With certain people this coolness of temperament is of a moderate cast and takes the name of phlegm.

Phlegm is a defense against visible emotion. It is not hypocrisy or falsehood, for the phlegmatic utter no sentiment contrary to that which they fill. They are content not to let anything transpire of the causes of their agitation. One may compare a phlegmatic man to a thick veil under which the play of the features, and under this the acts of the mind, are dissembled.

Hypocrisy resembles a dead wall covered with lying advertisements.

Phlegm is this dead wall wholly denuded of these. We can conjecture what it conceals, but in no case can we accuse it of saying anything contrary to truth.

Coolness of temperament, too often confounded with phlegm, differs from it in the sense that it is in need of some special circumstance for its manifestation. It is founded above all in quick decision, the result of brief deduction, of which the characteristics are prudence and just appreciation. In the ordinary circumstances of life coolness of temperament is known as circumspection.

Circumspection is very precise in its affairs. It is a quality that draws its origin from strength of character, for it goes straight to its desired object. Thanks to circumspection one will avoid pronouncing upon a thing until he has made a thorough study of it in its possible combinations. Further, it is the trait that supplies the necessary clearness requisite to guaranty engagements made beforehand by furnishing pretexts for momentary abstention, if such be profitable for the business in hand.

And since we have made use of the word clearness, let us say something about its concern in business affairs.

It is the gift that permits us to foresee the consequences of the act dictated by coolness of temperament. Clearness can not exist without strength of character, for it is the latter which supplies the willpower essential to getting rid of the burdensome considerations that keep us from discussing the right course.

Clearness is like a light brought into the midst of darkness; as the illumination permits of distinguishing each object lost in shadow, clearness shows all the motives detaching themselves from the mists of the principal theme, no matter how involved. In case of possible disaster it will show in a strong light the disadvantages of some act that may be fatal, tho it seem to us beneficent. It is above all a preventive quality; it does not determine, it points out, and thus serves to caution us against possible impending danger.

Before seizing an object we direct toward it and what surrounds it the rays of the lamp, examining everything in the light And when we have fixt our choice we like to convince ourselves by means of minute scrutiny that it is worth while.

Here ends the role of clearness, whose place is now taken by perspicacity.

This is the quality that permits of discerning the real value of the object, or its utility.

Prudence now intervenes in order to permit us to envisage the disadvantages incurred in the resolution.

Discernment will enable us to see the advantages that may flow from it.

Reason provides us with the faculty of comparing and weighing these advantages to the end that we may know exactly which to choose.

Deduction permits us to infer their consequences, the probability of which will be in accordance with the strictness of the mental operation.

Finally, coolness of temperament, the synthesis of all these qualities, will appear upon the scene to aid us to put in practise the resolutions they have inspired.

These resolutions may be important or simply may concern the humblest questions of daily life; they will exhibit an intimate relation with coolness of temperament.

Strength of character will be found valuable in that it will put the lid down upon the effervescence of those who waste themselves in words. Such as these give copious utterance to puerile wishes, but miscarry lamentably when it is a question of making them good. Others allow themselves to be carried away by a too-apparent frankness and are incapable of that urbanity which is the necessary condition of carrying on all business.

Urbanity can be practised in all circumstances of social life. It consists in a form of politeness which by no means excludes firmness, but has a way of recovering it agreeably. It is suggestive of the well-known image of the iron hand in a velvet glove. By using politeness it is possible to refuse what is injurious to our interests without hurting the one we address.

Urbanity is the brilliant covering of the bitter pill. We are all made so that an insipid medicament presented to us in pleasant guise has more attraction for us than has some dainty of repulsive aspect.

Strength of character in business is the appanage of those who are accustomed to call in logic in their decisions; which decisions being unembarrassed by the feeble sentiment that is characteristic of the weak, always bear the ear-mark of truth.

In cultivating logic, that is to say the art of reasoning, there is less chance of being deceived and precious time is saved, for he who gives himself up to tergiversations may be regarded in the light of a spendthrift. Moreover, those who cultivate logic, by compelling their minds to the exercise of thought soon become of the class known as prudent. The habit of rapid reflection opens to them horizons that must always remain cloud to those of feeble will, with the result that they can always create for themselves opportunities of wide import. They are the sort of whom it is said, "everything succeeds with them."

One might add that if success comes to them it is because they know how to gain and keep it themselves instead of uncomfortably waiting for it to come from some one else.

10

Strength of Character in Everyday Life

Individual happiness is always in direct ratio to the efforts made to obtain it. Discipline, self-control, the awakening in ourselves of the proper condition of mind to attain to success in our pursuits—these in brief *resume* constitute the chief desire of all.

All do not use the same formula in their aspirations. But there is no one that does not tend more or less actively toward some achievement. This achievement may consist of a series of accomplishments all of which concur to produce the general end in view; at times, however, it is a question of but one decisive act from which should flow some profitable result. In daily life, moreover, the first case is the most frequent one, the second coming solely as an exception.

It is rarely needful to enter upon a grave resolution, but we should in the day's course resolve on a series of minute determinations whose multiplicity constitutes the directing force.

For a woman the education of her children, their

maintenance, the cares of the home, the ordering of meals, surveillance of servants and their maintenance and wages are all occasions for developing qualities of patience, perseverance, judgment and perspicacity, all of which constitute strength of character.

Upon the accomplishment of these obscure duties depend most often the peace and harmony of life. They have a preponderant influence upon a man's state of mind; for accordingly as he is well or badly served, accordingly as the character of his surroundings is congenial or otherwise, he will come to love or dislike his home. Outside of internal disputes that trouble the existence of all who have to undergo them, there is a species of constant agitation that disposes us to unreasonable nervousness and interferes seriously with our duties. Strength of character banished from the home relinquishes it to reasonless impulsiveness, which then comfortably installs itself, bringing in its train the procession of disagreements and moral disorders, upon which sane reason, tossed about and buffeted from all sides, quickly makes its escape without intending to return.

Veracity, integrity, and goodness, which form the essence of strong character, do not find themselves at ease among acts that lack reflection.

Firmness of purpose is a power that can be exercised as well in the ordinary acts of life as in those inspired by circumstances of grave nature. All educators ought to let this truth sink into their minds.

The education that tends to moral virility is a question of example. Children always adopt the character and ways of those who direct them. Even in cases where they are rebellious they always incline to introduce into the very contradictions they fight for the elements and ways of life that they have learned from their teacher. Example is one of the most real instructors that it is possible to conceive of; its silent and persistent power betrays itself in habits of mind, unconscious at times, which blends the life of pupil and master in such community of thought and feeling that it is always difficult to change it.

It is therefore indispensable to give to children from early youth principles of strong character which later on will be seen to develop to advantage. And to fortify the lesson example is invaluable.

It is apparent how strength of character in parents can influence children for good. It may transform their whole life by arming them against deceptions and reverses. Often it prevents misfortune from coming; but even in case of its arrival those who have been brought up in the school of strong principle will know how to accept it without weakness.

This firmness of character will prevent many a disaster in the morning of life; it will prove to be a barrier against the allurements at the bottom of which is found nothing but disappointment and disgust, and will enable counsels of reason to prevail with those whom the impetuosity of twenty-one may have led into the pathways frequented by vice.

Later on it will again intervene, the time having come to make choice of a career. It is then that strength of character becomes an office of daily application. The principal effort resolved upon, the career chosen, the grave resolution taken, it becomes a question of "making good." Only feeble spirits are content to look upon the bright side of what attracts them. Strong characters take a kind of delight in stripping the object of desire of all ornament that may give it an aspect foreign to its nature. For these last there are therefore less deceptions; deceptions nevertheless will present themselves in goodly number and it is the part of strength of character to palliate them rather than have recourse to dissimulation.

Later on choice of a companion for the voyage of existence will give occasion for the developing of those sturdy qualities that should animate us all. Here sane reason should impose its laws upon us and it will be well to recall the celebrated axiom:

> "It is not by the ornaments at the ship's prow that the passengers are assured of safety."

There are cases where strength of character should lend us its powerful aid to resist the physical allurements that conceal moral defects.

Stoicism is not limited to contempt for physical suffering; at times it consists in the resolve to endure suffering of sentimental nature, the cause of which seems an unworthy one. Further, it is character that equips us with the strength to resist passions of small, demeaning nature, which at the turning-point of forty often assail those who have succeeded in warding them off in their youth.

Every one may be master of himself, but the law involves a different interpretation for each.

The exigencies of life demand from each one a different effort. An artizan can not be expected to do the work of a magistrate; a musician or a literary worker can not have the mind of a man who deals in realities dependent upon material effort.

There is a marked difference between the laws of reality and the laws of thought, considered in an ideal aspect. Nevertheless, the laws of this same thought, made up of true elements whence flow firm and directed determination, are valid for all.

We know that all contradictory judgments are tainted with falsehood. Weakness of character has the effect always of maiming reason, with the consequent result of producing contradictory decisions. It also engenders that pitiful means of defense, falsehood. Weak characters are rarely immune from this. It is a sort of necessity for them; it is the way they remedy or think they remedy the insufficiency of their means of defense. Lack of intelligence does not permit them to appreciate the consequences incurred by their want of frankness. It is more difficult to support a falsehood than to face the risks of truth.

The habit of frankness permits of viewing an event in all its phases and of guarding against painful surprizes. It is to be remarked that liars are seldom in good faith with themselves. The habit of perverting truth makes them less delicate in regard to sincerity in general. Also it is not a rare thing to see liars dupe themselves involuntarily just as they consciously seek to dupe others. This habit is in everyday life the cause of frequent disorders, and constant disputes. The custom of dissembling everything always proceeds from weakness of character which thinks thus to suppress difficulties. The liar does not reflect that the fact of destroying certain obstacles by the word does not prevent them from subsisting in reality, and that the desired ignorance in which it is sought to keep the interested makes them neglect the necessary precautions for their safety. Proneness to lying in the little incidents of daily life has its source in two opposite sentiments, both of which proceed from weakness of character. The first is the strong desire to play a part. One who is possest with this, not feeling in himself the strength of will that gives the necessary aptitude for great result, transforms for his own benefit everything that he comes in contact with. He appears on the scene, looks around, takes in everything, and speaks his thoughts. Very well; these things are always to his advantage, and he always overwhelms his hearers with the idea of his importance. The whole thing usually ends most pitifully for the deceiver, his deceptions always being quickly discovered.

The other sentiment consists in mental idleness which looks with horror upon every sort of complication, even the most insignificant. Weaklings who are afflicted with this defect will lie to escape the slightest trouble.

A young man given to lying, a weakling, was sent by his father to get some information from his former employers concerning one about to be engaged. Instead of taking the usual measures the young man found it more simple to give his father excellent recommendations which the latter did not think of verifying. Some months later a deficit in the accounts attracted his attention; the employees were watched, and it was found the newcomer was the author of the thefts. Imagine the agitation of the father, who, before taking stern measures, demanded an interview with the delinquent's former employers who had so cheerfully given excellent references. Great was his stupefaction on learning that they had discharged this employee for cause and had never heard any more about him, much less given him references.

Habitual lying has not always such grievous immediate results as this, but it has another kind that is not less reprehensible; it creates mistrust and destroys confidence, upon which harmony is based. With doubt is born a sort of contempt for the person in whose word it is impossible to trust.

In time, discredit attaints his very nature and it becomes impossible for him to give his mind to any real achievement, all the more because he does not know the value of noble things and no longer wants to be of those who live in the light of day, and whose reliance is placed upon truth and character without which no enterprise can have hope of success.

11

Happiness and Strength of Character

It is an absurd theory which places happiness in an effortless life.

Each one here below has his formula, and it is long indeed since the sage uttered this thought: "What makes the happiness of one does not at all make that of another."

The meaning of thc maxim has been trusted by those who like to see in it a sort of *revanche* of fate by which some are permitted to profit at the expense of others. We should like to believe that the author of this proverb has really deserved the title of thinker and that he only desired to express this fact: "The conception of happiness is not the same for all."

There are those whose ambition is limited by a life of peace and harmony. Others crave brilliant triumphs and find happiness in honor and wealth alone. For certain persons honors and brilliant existence are the sole desirable aim. To reach the height of these diverse ambitions but one means exists—conquest. In order to conquer there is but one means available, strength of character, which gives the willpower to conquer. By virtue of strength of character we may solve the problem of happy labor which for nine-tenths of us means contentment. We have seen in a preceding chapter that everybody, under one form or another, is obliged to do some kind of work. Formerly sovereigns with their ministers worked just like artizans. All depended upon manual labor, all worked and had to work.

Work done in a sullen way doubles the difficulty of effort, making it so hard at times that we hesitate to attempt it. Gayety, the offspring of character, gives elasticity to the mind and lessens the sense of difficulty. Work done sullenly is nearly, always unproductive, and insipidity of effort supervenes disagreeably upon the ordinary conditions of happiness. To do what has to be done with cheerfulness and to apply oneself to it earnestly is the secret of all felicity. If we are not careful the little *ennuis* of life, untransformed by intelligent action, end by invading our very lives and leaving no place for joy to penetrate. They are like fine flakes of snow which separately have no consistency, dissolving as quickly as they fall, but whose accumulation means insuperable obstacles and even formidable avalanches.

Herein is exprest the trait of those who are ignorant of strength of character; they allow themselves to be dominated by the trifling bustle of daily life instead of transforming it by a use of willpower into events whose ordered course might give a vivid interest to daily life.

The essential condition of happiness consists above all in the power of willing it.

We do not mean to assert that the mere desire to be happy smoothes over all difficulties and does away with all the unpleasantness of life. But he who encourages his own life with a will for happiness always discovers in it reasons for contentment which hitherto have escaped his observation. We say *his own life* and not that of others. There is no more certain sign of feeble character than is the propensity to regard another's lot preferable to one's own. If the comparison is made in good faith it will generally be found that a grievous mistake has been made, and that to exchange some good of our own for that of our neighbour would be a bad bargain.

Happiness, moreover, is a question of relativity. In order to appreciate it we must take account of origin, habits, situation, age, etc. What makes for the happiness of a young man would be a matter of indifference to a man of maturity, while an old man will find pleasure in occupations that leave the latter indifferent. What would seem like want to a man used to wealth would appear like a desirable competence to a man unspoiled by it. Finally idleness, the avowed aim of so much effort, becomes for the one who realizes it a source of *ennui* bordering on sadness. Those who are endowed with strength of character are never ignorant of the fact; happiness is everywhere if one knows the secret of placing it in the accomplishment of a task.

Idleness, by annihilating desire, destroys interest in life. It is an unfailing source from which feeble souls draw the discouragement which makes them cry out on happiness; of such are the barren regrets concerning an act whose consequences can not be changed.

An Oriental proverb says: "It is better to yearn for a cabin than to mourn for a palace." And it is impossible not to admire the virile character of the mind that dictated the thought. Desire for a cabin implies a hard struggle to possess one, a series of efforts that are necessary to become its owner, a sustained daily interest in the life of him who devotes himself to its conquest. Regretting a palace amounts to an avowal that we are reconciled to the fate that has befallen us and are without hope of changing it. The word barren as applied to regret is no sterile phrase. Nothing can be more fruitless than regrets. Nothing is more opposed to the survival of happiness. He who calls himself happy proclaims the plenitude of actual content-ment and yet has hope of bettering his best.

But he who consumes himself in vain regret gives the lie to the happiness of the magical present and uses up his strength in deploring conditions that nothing can change.

There is one circumstance, however, in which regret may bear actual fruit. It is when we call character to our aid in order to make a thorough examination of the causes which have provoked disaster. The examination may be made by means of a single consideration; try to discover the vice in the events which have brought about the incident we deplore. If the *denouement* is due to lack of cleverness, to carelessness, or certain personal defects, regret for them will not be fruitless, since they will involve a resolution not to fall into the same errors a second time. There is no sense in regretting a past event unless we make a resolution not to relapse into the same faults which were produced by it.

Another cause of happiness is health.

Now health can not exist without strength of character, a quality which saves us from excess and enables us to take care of ourselves. No one will question that it is impossible to enjoy the happiness that life concedes us if suffering comes to spoil every hour. But are not we ourselves frequently the authors of this suffering?

Excess at table disposes some to ills of suggestion that poison their existence. Others consume their health in nightly fatigues and spend in sleep, often a besotted kind, the finest hours of the day, hours that seem to them insipid and disagreeable because they see them in the lens of their own lassitude. Others perhaps, suffer from some evil that the body ignores, but which, none the less, may be deepseated.

Then there are the disillusioned, those who have demanded too much of happiness, and have not known enough to be content with what was given them. The trouble comes nearly always from feebleness of character, which delights to nourish itself with illusions whose false reflection dazzles them to the point of hiding from them the necessity for effort. If they were sincere they would confess that the poverty of the result is in direct proportion to the energy expended. All realization, barring unforeseen accidents, responds exactly to the sum of activity deployed.

To this must be joined cleverness, however. And this is still dependent upon strength of character. A plan, to be well conceived, demands attention, analysis and good sense. How can these be expected of one so weak as not to be able to endure the thought of assiduity? It is only persons of strong willpower who devote to the elaboration of a task the amount of moral and physical activity that it requires. Thus they are rarely seen to become victims of the shameful conclusions that the weak know too well. They are not indeed under the wing of that unforeseen felicity that is so seldom known, but this kind of happiness is the exception, and it must have been in alluding to people of character that one who had achieved distinguished success remarked:

"We have the happiness that we deserve."